MY GUIDING STAR

RICHARD J. MIHANS II

ISBN 979-8-89112-704-3 (Paperback)
ISBN 979-8-89112-706-7 (Hardcover)
ISBN 979-8-89112-705-0 (Digital)

Covenant Books
11661 Hwy 707
Murrells Inlet, SC 29576
www.covenantbooks.com

To Helen Lucas, my beloved grandma—
half my heart. To Anna, my cherished
mother—the other half of my heart.

Vassar Hospital

The night I was born, the world was blanketed in snow. Dad braved the snowy, stormy night to get Mom and me to the hospital.

Ten minutes later, I arrived. Mom says that as soon as I was born, Grandma held me in her arms, gave me my name, and whispered, "Richie, see those tiny diamonds in the sky? Those are stars, and they're here for you. They're twinkling, winking, and blinking because they are so excited to be here for your first birthday party!" Of course, the rest of my family must have been asleep to miss the stars coming to my birthday party. They say they don't remember that happening, but Grandma says it's true, so I know it is.

CONGRATS
It's a boy!
It's a boy!

"The thunder and lightning are scary, Grandma! I wish the stars were shining. Why do they go away on the scariest nights when we need them most? I feel lost without their twinkling, winking, and blinking light."

"Oh, they're there, Richie. But like us, they need to stay warm and dry until the storm passes. Soon, our diamonds will come back out to play. When they do, they'll be shining brightly just like always. You'll see!" And Grandma was right! The stars came back out as soon as the storm passed. Stars always do.

On clear nights, when the stars were twinkling, winking, and blinking, we'd sit on the hood of Dad's car and gaze at the diamonds in the sky, sharing secrets and dreams we hoped would come true.

At school, I learned about constellations and their magical stories. I rushed home to tell Grandma about the North Star and Harriet Tubman, the brave hero who led many enslaved people to freedom by following the stars. Grandma smiled and said, 'It's true. Stars can be our guides."

We made wishes on shooting stars, believing our dreams would come true. At night, we sang 'Starlight, Star Bright,' wishing upon stars for adventures. We always looked for shooting stars because Grandma said that's where our wishes lived. "Even Jiminy Cricket knew," she would say, "that wishes upon stars are the most magical of all."

STAR STUDENTS
M E
TARS!!
Harriet Tubman

New York
North Carolina

One day, Dad came home excited and said, "I couldn't pass up this amazing job opportunity." Because of that, we would have to move far away—to another state, twelve hours from Grandma! I couldn't imagine being so far from her. We'd never been that far apart. I was so mad at Dad for taking us away and so sad about moving. I told Grandma it made me feel sick to my stomach, like I wanted to throw up, and that I would be lost without her. *Lost!*

And even though I knew Grandma was sad too, she tried to make me smile by saying that this new adventure would be exciting. "We'll tell each other new secrets and share dreams we haven't imagined yet. And if you ever feel lost," she said, "just look up at the night sky. Find the brightest star that's twinkling, winking, and blinking, and know that's me. I'll be the brightest diamond in the night sky, guiding you."

PELLEGRINO MOVERS
NOTHING WE CAN'T MOVE!
Family Room
Kitchen
Family Room
Fragile

When we moved away, Grandma was still there, guiding me. When I felt lost and needed to see her, she would buy me a plane ticket. The coolest part was taking those flights to her home, riding with the stars to see her.

Time flew by, and I grew up. Even though I remembered all the twinkling, winking, and blinking from those magnificent diamonds in the sky, I got so busy with life, as teenagers and young adults sometimes do, that I forgot to stop and look at the night sky as I used to.

1st
Place
Seniors

Then one day, Mom called me with the news I dreaded hearing the most. Grandma was very sick, and now she needed a guide.

I rushed as fast as I could to get to Grandma. I stayed by her side, just like she'd always been there for me.

And even though I followed every order the doctor gave; she just wasn't getting better. So, I stayed with her, loved her, and told her she was the brightest diamond in the sky and that I'd keep her warm and dry should a storm come anytime soon.

With tears in her eyes, she said, "I don't want to sleep, Richie. I'm afraid I'll miss the stars." Just as she said this, we saw a brightness from the window, and a shooting star streaked across the sky. Grandma smiled and said in a hoarse voice, "Make a wish on the shooting star, my little star."

I closed my eyes as tightly as I could and made a heart wish as large as the night sky. As we locked eyes, she barely whispered again, "I'm afraid I'll miss the stars."

But before I could tell her that she was the twinkling, winking, and blinking part of the stars, she was gone. Words can't describe the heart-wrenching pain of losing my grandma. Maybe you've felt this before— the unbearable loss of someone you love deeply. It's a pain that leaves you empty, realizing how much you loved them only when they're gone. It's the kind of sorrow that makes you realize that things can change in an instant and that when someone's gone, there's no replacing them. Nothing could ease this pain, and I didn't even try. This is the profound sadness you feel when you've lost someone who is irreplaceable.

25

As time went by, the intensity of those feelings numbed somewhat, and I began to just live with it, accepting that's how it was going to be.

Then the holidays came, and I felt that deep sadness creep back because I remembered just how much Grandma had loved them. But miraculously, as I looked at the Christmas tree and saw the twinkling star on top, I immediately thought to look out the window and saw the most beautiful winking and blinking star. I thought of my grandma and realized that keeping a little bit of that pain was okay because it kept her memory alive. It was also important to tuck the rest away and enjoy life again. In that moment, I felt a sense of ease and comfort because I understood: even when stars go away, they never leave us, because they shine in our hearts forever.

The end.

About the Author

Dr. Richard J. Mihans II was born in Hyde Park, New York, but mostly grew up in Raleigh, North Carolina, where he enjoyed springs and summers at Atlantic Beach and autumns and winters in the Appalachian Mountains. He taught the fifth and sixth grades in the Piedmont region of North Carolina. Richard now resides just outside of New Orleans, Louisiana, where he lives with his amazing partner and comrade, Rafe, as well as their beloved pet fur pals: Dan "Jean," the most beautiful hound dog ever, and Chester, their orange tabby cat who likes to eat, sleep, and boss their new kitten, Norman, who is into everything!

Richard, a senior professor of education enjoys teaching teachers at Tulane University, loves to travel the world when he can, and, of course, counts his lucky stars for this amazing life that God has provided him and his family and friends.